Problem? What Problem?

Dealing Effectively with Impediments using Agile Thinking with Problem-solving Practices

Ben Linders

ISBN 9789492119254

Leanpub

This is a Leanpub book. Leanpub empowers authors and publishers with the Lean Publishing process. Lean Publishing is the act of publishing an in-progress ebook using lightweight tools and many iterations to get reader feedback, pivot until you have the right book and build traction once you do.

Tweet This Book!

Please help Ben Linders by spreading the word about this book on Twitter!

The suggested tweet for this book is:

Great new book on effectively handling impediments - Problem? What problem? by @BenLinders

The suggested hashtag for this book is #impediments.

Find out what other people are saying about the book by clicking on this link to search for this hashtag on Twitter:

#impediments

Also By Ben Linders

What Drives Quality

Getting Value out of Agile Retrospectives

Waardevolle Agile Retrospectives

Welchen Wert Agile Retrospektiven liefern

Tirer profit des rétrospectives agiles

Obtendo Valor de Retrospectivas Ágeis

Ottieni il meglio dalle tue Retrospettive Agili

Извлекаем пользу из Agile-ретроспектив

Obteniendo valor de las Retrospectivas ágiles

从敏捷回顾中收获价值

アジャイルふりかえりから価値を生み出す − 日本語版

Wartościowe Retrospekcje Agile

Continuous Improvement

Αποκομίζοντας αξία από τα Agile Retrospectives

Khai thác giá trị Agile Retrospective

Jak zvýšit přínos agilních retrospektiv

The Agile Self-assessment Game

Agile Manifesto Retrospectives Questions Cards

Agile Testing Coaching Cards

Agile Retrospectives Bingo

Agile Retrospective Smells Cards

Contents

Foreword

As a consultant, I only work with people who have problems. (No one calls a consultant when things go well.)

And, many of my clients confuse their problems (what Ben calls impediments) with the *signals* of the actual problem. That initial frame—differentiate between impediment and signal—sets the tone for the rest of the book.

Ben masterfully detangles the various ways problems expose themselves to the teams. And, he includes several ideas about adapting existing practices to help *your* team. He recommends you think of practices as patterns, not recipes.

The middle part of this book addresses many of the agile frameworks and how to challenge framework thinking. Too many people in the agile community think frameworks are recipes. All you need to do is apply the framework or "cook" the organization according to the recipe and you'll succeed. Ben (and I) have not seen that approach succeed.

Instead, Ben recommends we look for those signals. Once we see those signals, we can reconsider how to recognize and resolve our impediments. Ben addresses several common antipatterns, such as a person removing the impediment *for* the team. He recommends joint problem-solving—the team, team leadership, and the managers—for impediment removal. I agree with him. I rarely see the team "hero" succeed alone.

Ben spends a significant portion of the book on impediments beyond the team level. These systemic impediments challenge any agile team to succeed, never mind several teams acting in concert. Ben leads us through ways to recognize these problems, how to explain the impacts of these impediments, and how we might start to resolve these problems.

In the last section, Ben suggests several reasonable actions to improving our problem-solving abilities. I particularly liked the section, "Don't Try to Change Everything at Once." Too many of my clients make that mistake and get stuck in all the changes.

Use this book to add more capabilities to your problem-solving toolkit. Integrate Ben's tips and keys as you read and you'll start to recognize your signals and impediments—and resolve them.

Johanna Rothman, Consultant and Writer, author of *Modern Management Made Easy, books 1-3*

Preface

This is the first book specifically about dealing with impediments using agile thinking with problem-solving practices. In this book, I explain why dealing with impediments matters. The book also provides approaches for you to effectively handle impediments in teams and beyond the teams. I'm also sharing experience stories from my practice.

This book is for agile teams, Scrum masters, tech leads, agile coaches, consultants, developers and testers, project managers, line managers, and CxOs; basically, anyone who is looking for an effective way to handle impediments or support people in doing that.

You may wonder how I came up with the title of this book *Problem? What Problem?*. When you know how to effectively deal with problems, then problems aren't a problem anymore for you. And that is exactly what this book aims to do: Help people developing their problem-solving skills and learn how to apply practices to effectively handle impediments.

This book doesn't intend to teach you what agile is or show you how to become agile. In essence, it is about dealing with impediments when you are working in an agile way. This book also explores how you can handle impediments using an agile mindset and thinking. It's about agile applied to problem-solving. Hence the subtitle *Dealing Effectively with Impediments using Agile Thinking with Problem-solving Practices*.

This book includes information about the Impediment Coaching Cards and the Impediment Board Game. You can download these Agile Coaching Tools for a nominal fee in my webshop.

I based this book on my experience as a developer, tester, team leader, project manager, quality manager, process manager, consultant, coach, trainer, and adviser in Agile, Lean, Quality, and Continuous Improvement. This book dives into problem solving and impediments, viewing them from different perspectives and provides ideas, suggestions, practices, and experiences that will help you to become more effective in dealing with impediments.

I want to thank the many reviewers of my book for investing time and coming up with ideas to improve it (in alphabetical order): Mike Caddell, Tom Cagley, Glaudia Califano, Sunish Chabba, Paddy Corry, Scott Duncan, Madhavi Ledalla, Erwin van Maren, Jonathan Orgel, Kamil Puk, Annemiek Quirijns, Srinath Ramakrishnan, Carina Silfverduk, and David Spinks. Thank you for proofreading earlier versions of the book and providing many suggestions. Your feedback has helped me to make this a better book!

A big thanks to Johanna Rothman for writing the foreword for this book. The first time that I have met her in person was in 2003 at the Software Management & Applications of Software Measurement conference. She was a co-host and I did a session on the business benefits of root cause analysis. Johanna has a knack of coming up with practical solutions for solving problems in her books, articles, and newsletters. Over the years she has inspired me with great ideas that I used for solving problems; now I'm sharing what I'm using in this book.

I love to hear your experiences in dealing with impediments. Feel free to email me at benlinders@gmail.com!

Finally, I would like to thank all the people who invest time to read my blog and comment on the articles. Your feedback helps me to increase my understanding of topics that I write about and makes it worthwhile for me to keep blogging!

Ben Linders
July 2020

Introduction

Over the years, development and delivery of software have become more continuous and flow-based. Faster throughput is crucial to deliver value and get feedback from customers.

Agile defines impediments as problems that slow down teams or keep teams from getting work done. They are an obstruction or obstacle, something that hinders people. Impediments have an impact on the flow of work, they inhibit delivery of value.

Impediments need to be dealt with. This can be hard. Having the right skills and applying them using suitable practices can make a significant difference.

This book is about dealing effectively with impediments using agile thinking with problem-solving practices. It explores how teams and organizations can deal with problems themselves. By doing that, they become better in self-organizing the way that they do their work. The book also provides solutions for dealing with impediments beyond the team level.

My Experience with Solving Problems

Throughout my career, I became more and more interested in problem-solving. From my early days as a developer through to my later roles as a team leader and then as a project manager, solving problems was a major part of my work. Over time I became good at solving problems by practicing it.

To develop my problem-solving skills, I've read a lot of books on how to deal with problems. Trying out things from these books, I learned to analyze problems, decide what to do and how to do it, and take action to get problems out of the way. In this book, I share my learnings and experiences.

Scrum and other agile frameworks use the word "impediment" for anything that keeps teams from getting work done. Those are basic problems that need to be solved. The big difference with agile however is that it expects people to solve their own problems. So, everybody needs problem-solving skills. But how to develop them?

I started looking for ways to blend the agile mindset and principles with existing problem-solving practices. My aim was to adapt what's there for using it within modern software development, and show how these practices fit into Scrum, XP, Kanban, or any other agile framework.

 I'm an active blogger at www.benlinders.com. On my blog, I share my experiences on agile and lean topics, including how to handle impediments in teams using agile thinking and practices.

Meanwhile, my work had changed. Since 2009 I'm a one-person company doing many different things to help people, teams, and companies become better in developing and delivering high-quality software products and services.

In 2015 I published a blog series on handling impediments. The articles provided an approach and many practical agile tips. Being hands-on, these articles became very popular. I used them as a starting point for this book.

I train and coach. I advise teams and organizations. I write books. I also speak and give workshops at conferences.

 In my workshops, I teach people how to deal with impediments to truly become self-organized. I created cards with signals about possible impediments. I use them in exercises where people practice recognizing potential problems and learning how to handle them.

Finding out that there's a limit to how much traveling I can do, I decided to go on my own "agile scaling and digitalization" journey.

 My books, games, exercises, workshops and remote training, and other agile coaching tools that I use myself in my workshops and advice work are available as digital downloads for a nominal fee in my webshop at benlinders.com/shop/.

I decided to take the cards from my workshops, turn them into a product, and release them as Impediment Coaching Cards. This is the first-ever agile coaching tool for dealing with impediments.

Although these cards and the way I use them to help people to develop their impediment handling skills can contribute a lot already, I wanted to take it one step further by turning it into a real serious game.

At the XP Days Benelux 2018 I played a board game where people in teams learned how to deal with impediments. I based the game on the famous Game of Goose board game (in Dutch: Ganzenbord) where I turned it from a competitive game into a collaborative game. I got great feedback at the XP Days which I used to update the game.

 This game is available to the world in digital format as The Impediment Board Game. You can download it for a nominal fee.

Having a set of short articles and two agile coaching tools on impediments I started thinking about what more I could do to help the world to become better in dealing with impediments. Noticing that my third book The Agile Self-assessment Game, released early 2019, has become very popular I decided to share my knowledge and experience in dealing with impediments also in a book.

And that's why I wrote *Problem? What Problem? - Dealing Effectively with Impediments using Agile Thinking and Practices.*

What's in This Book

This book provides ideas with solutions for dealing effectively with impediments.

In the chapter Problem Solving and Impediments I explore why being able to deal with impediments matters for agile teams.

Dealing with Impediments in Teams provides an approach for recognizing and analyzing impediments and deciding on the actions.

In the intermezzo Agile Frameworks and Methods I discuss what Scrum, SAFe, LeSS, Scrum@Scale, and other agile methods provide for dealing with impediments.

Handling Impediments Beyond the Team Level dives into systemic organizational issues or problems that hinder multiple teams or need management support to solve them.

The chapter Increasing your Effectiveness provides many practices and tips to become better in dealing with impediments.

In Agile Coaching Tools for Impediments I describe games, coaching cards, and exercises, to improve impediment handling capabilities and skills. Training and Support explores workshops for assessing and improving your agility.

The Bibliography provides an extensive list of books, articles, and links, that you can use to acquire in-depth knowledge for dealing with impediments.

This is a practical book with many techniques and ideas to apply in your specific situations. It aims to support professionals that want to improve their impediment handling skills.

Using the Book

There are many suggestions and pieces of advice in this book that help you to deal with impediments effectively. I marked them as tips with a key symbol:

Try those tips that look suitable and see if they work for you. If they do, great! If not, try another one.

I also share stories and cases from my own experience. They are from organizations and teams that I have worked with, as well as from my training and coaching sessions:

Stories, cases, and examples, have a user symbol. They inspire you to think about what you might do.

Reading suggestions for this book and information about additional tools, books, and services, are marked with QR codes or an exclamation mark:

Registration at benlinders.com/problem-what-problem gives you access to supporting materials, games, and workshops, that can help you to improve your impediment handling skills. Highly recommended!

Register your book today to get a discount on the impediment games!

With plenty of ideas, suggestions, examples, and practical cases on impediments, this book will help you to become more effective in dealing with impediments.

Problem Solving and Impediments

Agile emphasizes establishing teams and giving them whatever they need to do their work. Teams will face problems in their daily work. Agile calls these problems impediments.

> An impediment is anything that slows people down and needs to be dealt with.

Impediments can be something in the way of working, be it processes, tools, or organizational rules or structures. They slow down teams or block the delivery of products or services.

Impediments can also be something cultural or structural that inhibits the team from learning something about their customers or hinders them from collaborating with their stakeholders. They can make it difficult for teams to find out how they are doing, or block them while improving their way of working.

This chapter explores what solving problems is all about. It defines what impediments are and are not. Finally, it explains why being able to deal with impediments matters for agile teams.

Impediments and Signals

Earlier I defined impediments as anything that slows people down and needs to be dealt with. This is a pretty broad definition. Let's take a look at some examples of impediments and things that I wouldn't call an impediment but a signal that tells us there might be a problem.

Examples of impediments are:

- Build time that keeps increasing
- Toxic behavior from people that you have to work with
- Networks or cloud-based systems that are failing
- Power outages
- Frequent conflicts between people
- Accumulating technical debt
- Situations where people object to or find it difficult to work with other people
- Elephants in the room that nobody dares to mention
- Many test cases that are failing
- Unavailability of people
- Difficulties to contact people when you need them
- Organizational procedures making it difficult to do your work
- Bad coffee
- Lots of discussions about everything while making no progress
- Having to work in a sick building
- Situations that cause people to remain silent most of the time
- Personal problems that people bring to work
- The office police
- Teams depending on other teams or departments

There are many more things that can be an impediment, these are just some examples to give you an idea of problems that can be slowing down people.

As you see in the above list, it can be technical things, organizational issues, the way that people behave, dynamics between people, the culture or structure of the company, the way the company is managed, etc.

Many things cause impediments. To solve impediments you can explore the root causes. For instance, if your technical debt is increasing, architects and developers can investigate what is causing it to grow and what is blocking people from reducing it.

When people are being slowed down by an impediment, there are usually signals that tell you that this is happening. A signal is not an impediment, it is an indicator telling you that you might have an impediment.

Examples of signals are:

- Things take longer than expected
- People are complaining
- Unclear user stories/requirements
- A lack of collaboration in the company
- Team members that are stuck and don't ask for help
- Skipping the retrospective
- People seem to be avoiding somebody
- Code integration issues
- Customers who are unhappy with your products
- Important work that is not being picked up
- Stakeholders that are complaining

If you are unsure if what you have is a signal or an impediment, start by asking yourself why this is happening. If that leads you to something that could be causing multiple problems, then you might be looking at an impediment.

A signal might also lead you to one or more of the root causes of an impediment. Asking why helps to learn more about the impediment which will make it easier for you to solve it.

In the section recognizing impediments I'll explore how you can pick up such signals and dig deeper to find the underlying impediments.

Dealing with Impediments

The fifth principle from the manifesto for agile software development states:

Build projects around motivated individuals.
Give them the environment and support they need,
and trust them to get the job done.

When I mention agile in this book, I do not have a specific framework or model in mind. Agile for me is a result-oriented way of working together based on self-organization.

Over the years I have learned that handling impediments is a key value for all teams and organizations to increase their agility. Regardless of the methods or frameworks used or how it's called, problem-solving is an essential skill for all employees.

Different methods and frameworks use various terms when they talk about impediments.

Where some methods use other terms, like "bottleneck", "barrier" or "obstacle", for this book I use the terms "impediment" and "problem".

In this book, I consider blockers to be a special kind of impediment. A blocker is something that inhibits work completely and brings it to a halt.

Blockers are a subset from impediments: every blocker is an impediment, but most impediments are not blockers as often people will still be able to proceed when they face an impediment.

There Will Be Problems

An agile way of working doesn't guarantee that there will be no problems. Most probably there will be. Agile can help to identify problems, it tends to bring problems to the surface.

Agile didn't invent dealing with problems, nor do agile frameworks like Scrum tell you what to do about it. But when you work in an agile way, it's better to be prepared for problems once they become visible.

The strength of working in an agile way is that when a problem is there it will usually become visible. Often sooner than when you were using a traditional approach like waterfall.

Visualization means making things visible, things that people don't see or might have had different views on. Things made transparent and visual are easier for people to discuss and share their views on. This helps them to align their thinking and get a better understanding.

When you're working in an agile team, nobody will solve your problems for you.

Agile teams need to have the skills to deal with impediments to be effective. They need them to deliver products and services that satisfy the needs of their customers and stakeholders.

Teams need empowerment, autonomy, and trust to be able to deal with their impediments.

Agile Mindset and Thinking

If an organization is working in an agile way, their approach to solving problems should also be agile-based. It has to fit in and be congruent with the company's agile mindset to be effective.

What does problem-solving look like when we are using an agile mindset and agile thinking? Here's my view:

- Many problems relate to the way people work together. Where every person does the best they can, problems often arise when things come together. Problem-solving practices should help us to understand how individuals interact and to solve collaboration issues.
- There are often too many problems to solve. We need to focus our effort on solving impediments that have the biggest impact on outcomes. Solve the ones that affect our ability to deliver something that is working.
- Collaboration is key, not only within teams but also between teams and when working with stakeholders. Problem-solving practices should enable us to visualize the system and collaboratively look for solutions. They should engage people from the start and enable them to self-organize and come up with solutions that work for them.
- While we're working on a problem, things will change. We'll learn new things along the way. We will find out what works and what doesn't. Problem-solving needs to respond to change to be effective. We need to be flexible on what problem-solving practices to use and how to use them.

 The agile manifesto mentions the four key values: Individuals and Interactions, Working Software, Customer Collaboration, and Responding to Change. You may recognize them in the above view :-).

Where the problem-solving practices may not be new to you, applying them with agile thinking can make a significant difference.

 It's about being agile over doing agile. Not doing problem-solving practices by the book, but applying them so that they can blend in with the daily work and hence be more effective.

Agile Teams Deal with Problems Themselves

Agile teams are self-organized. They can and should decide how they want to do their work themselves.

Having the authority to decide comes with a responsibility; agile teams are responsible for doing their work in the best possible way, and should always be on the lookout for things to improve their way of working.

This is why the agile manifesto recommends teams to reflect and adjust their behavior. Agile teams can do agile retrospectives to reflect, learn, and become better in what they do.

Teams are responsible for their own way of working. That means that team members will have to work together to solve problems that their team is facing.

 Make sure that agile teams do not rely upon management to solve their problems.

Having to solve problems yourself may sound like a disadvantage. But it actually is an opportunity since it allows you to solve them in a way that is most suitable and effective for you.

Agile teams are empowered to decide on their own agile journey and way of working.

There will be problems that will require participation from people outside of the team in order to solve them. The team might need help from other teams, management, or maybe even from people outside the organization. The chapter handling impediments beyond the team level provides ideas on how teams can involve others and collaborate to solve problems.

 My advice to managers is to not solve problems for teams, but instead, be available and offer help. Leave it up to the team to decide how they want to solve their problems.

It's the teams' responsibility to pro-actively engage whoever is required to solve impediments. Waiting for someone else to solve their problems is shirking their responsibility.

We Can't Solve All Impediments

There are always impediments. Sometimes there are few, often there are many.

It's impossible to solve all impediments at once. Even if that was possible, new problems will appear.

 You will need to prioritize impediments to decide what to solve and what not to solve, or not solve now.

Examples of criteria for deciding which impediment to solve are:

- The priority of the work that the impediment impacts
- How much the impediment blocks the team
- Loss or waste caused by the impediment
- The amount of work needed to solve the impediment
- Dependencies between impediments
- Chance of success of solving the impediment
- Risk or uncertainties related to the way of solving the impediment
- The availability of skills needed to solve the impediment

Usually, it's not possible to gather all information. Most decisions are made with incomplete information.

Solving impediments is a continuous activity. It is part of the daily work of people, hence it makes sense for everybody to develop their problem-solving skills.

Dealing with Impediments in Teams

This chapter provides an approach for teams to effectively deal with impediments. It's supported by practices and examples to use in your daily work.

Handling impediments in teams consist of:

- Recognizing impediments.
- Understanding how they hinder teams.
- Exploring effective solutions to deal with them.
- Deciding how to solve and who takes action.

The "process" steps listed above may suggest doing one after another. That works well in most situations. But this is by no means intended to be a waterfall-like process.

Usually, the steps for handling impediments take little time. Sometimes teams can go through all steps within an hour or less. Different team members can also do steps in parallel while collaborating to align their results.

An impediment came up in one of my retrospectives with a dispersed team: Team members felt that they missed opportunities to chat about things not directly related to the work or team. Co-located teams would have such chats during lunch or at the coffee machine. We decided to add a "virtual coffee machine" to our Trello board. Directly after the retrospective, a picture of a coffee machine appeared, together with a first note ... many great discussions followed.

In the case of distributed teams, members can spend some time when being online together to clarify any questions or problems they may have. These meetings also help in building rapport among the members. They also help to build relationships between team members and improve team cohesiveness.

When your team works in an agile way they can do short-cycle improvements to deal with impediments. The aim is to decide when to solve problems. For example, to do it now or assign it to the next sprint (when using Scrum), or assign a suitable priority (when using Kanban).

 In one retrospective, the team agreed on an action point to change their way of working. In the sprint planning that they did on the same day, they identified new tasks and stopped doing activities that had not been effective. This solved their action point. Two weeks later at the end of the iteration, they did the next retrospective and concluded that things were going much better.

There are always possibilities to work on your impediments, for example:

- Teams can work on one or more impediments in their retrospectives. For instance, if they discover that they have had major problems that they need to get out of the way.
- Teams can do one or more of the steps during their daily meeting or afterward to handle the impediments that they have.
- If needed, teams can schedule a separate meeting to explore one or more impediments. Meeting facilitators can help teams coming up with actions to deal with them.

If teams appear to be stuck in one step they can decide to proceed to the next one. Then they should prepare themselves to go back and repeat the steps once they have more information.

Recognizing Impediments

Let's dive into the first step for dealing with impediments: picking up signals and recognizing impediments.

Recognizing that there might be an impediment is a very important step. Often there is only a signal, so you have to be a good listener to notice it and pick it up.

At the daily meeting, somebody mentioned that she thought that the story that she was working on was "done", but she said she wasn't sure. Instead of ignoring her remark and moving the story to done, I asked what made her unsure. It turned out that she had a question on how the feature will be used. After the meeting, she discussed it with the product owner and was able to properly finish the story.

The things below are examples of signals that you can hear on the work floor:

- The priorities are changing all the time, this isn't workable
- My work is done, I'm waiting for other people
- We don't have time to do this properly
- The R&D manager dropped in, we need to do other work
- I'm too busy, I can't join the daily meeting
- We can only deliver on time if we skip the retrospective

Be aware that the signals mentioned above are usually a symptom of deeper problems. They are not the problem itself (more on this in the section understanding how impediments hinder teams).

Signals aren't only what people say, they can also be what people do (or don't do). It can, for example, be subtle things in how people behave, how the work is being done, or how people collaborate.

 A signal that there's something that prevents the team from getting stories to done might be a story with an inordinately longer cycle time than other similar stories. It could be a story that isn't completed in the sprint as intended (for teams using Scrum). This signal might indicate that there's something wrong with the definition of their stories.

To recognize a possible impediment, you have to become good at spotting things. Quoting Yogi Berra I'd say that "you can observe a lot by just watching".

 One organization did evaluations at the end of each project. The evaluations revealed similar problems like insufficient time and lack of people. These problems often were there from the start of the project, but it usually took a couple of months before they were reported. People were so busy with their daily work that they couldn't step back to take distance and see what was actually happening in the project.

Where most teams are able to recognize blockers, they may miss out on impediments. Blockers are easier to spot as they stop an activity, where other types of impediments often (gradually) slow things down.

As a team member, it can help to stop what you are doing and take a look at what you are doing and how you are doing it. Watching can be enough, look at how you work together as a team, how you plan and track your work, the practices that you apply, and use any feedback that you have.

Do these signals mentioned before sound familiar? That wouldn't surprise me. When I teach teams to become more effective in handling impediments, I see a lot of nodding in the classroom when I mention such signals.

I created the Impediment Coaching Cards which I often use in my workshop. These cards contain sentences with signals that teams can discuss to identify and learn about possible impediments that they face.

There have been several times where somebody stated in one of my workshops that they heard or saw something similar to these signals yesterday or in the past week at work.

What I've learned is that, when you hear signals like the ones listed above, you need to stop and make time to dig deeper to find out what's really happening.

Sometimes I meet people that do not want to hear bad news. Some managers say to me, "I hired you to solve problems, not to bring them up!" But remember:

Be aware that ignoring problems doesn't make them go away.

If there's a problem, when would teams like to know? Usually as soon as possible, to limit potential damage and not waste time. Solving problems before they get out of hand is usually also cheaper and much more effective.

A practice recommended by some agile coaches is to maintain an impediment log or separate impediment board. I worry that such a way of separating impediments from the work that is being done may lead to giving a lower priority to solving those impediments. There should be only one backlog and one task board; impediments should be included to give them the attention they deserve.

There has to be a mindset in the organization that "having a problem is not a problem". As Jack Sparrow said in Pirates of the Caribbean:

> The problem is not the problem. The problem is your attitude about the problem. Do you understand?

Don't shoot the messenger! We should not blame people when they bring up problems. When people don't feel safe enough to bring up problems, you're missing out on key information, risks, or issues. Instead, embrace the messenger by fostering a generative culture where people feel safe to raise problems.

 At a conference that I attended, I heard a presenter state that "at our company, we never shoot the messenger, unless (s)he is late". Even in that case, I would not shoot the messenger, but I may want to do a root cause analysis to find out why it took so long.

Some problems teams can solve themselves, for other problems they will need help from outside of the team. But before we can decide who can take action, we first need to understand the problem. This is the topic of the next section.

Summing up, if teams want to deal with impediments then team members need to keep their ears and eyes open to catch any signals that are there. Make it very clear that people (inside or outside the team) can go to any team member if something is bothering them or when they see a problem.

Understanding How Impediments Hinder Teams

This section explores what teams can do to understand impediments and gain insight into the underlying problems.

When there's an impediment, teams have to invest time to really understand the situation at hand before coming up with solutions. When they have a thorough understanding of what's happening, solving a problem becomes a lot easier.

 My experience is that once you have a deep understanding of the situation at hand, solutions will be obvious. Analyzing a problem or situation is not waste, it's time well spent.

There are different possible approaches for improving the understanding of a problem:

- 5 times why or root cause analysis
- Mark blockers
- Work aging
- Brainstorming
- Mindmaps
- Fishbone diagrams
- Powerful or strength-based questions
- Cynefin framework
- Appreciative Inquiry
- Retrospectives
- Collect data and facts
- Define measurements

Here are my recommendations for using these approaches to better understand how your impediments are hindering teams.

Understanding Impediments:

If you think that the problem which you are discussing is a symptom rather than the cause, then teams can do a *5 times why or root cause analysis* to dig deeper into the issue to find the real causes. A cause-effect diagram is a great way to visualize a problem. Don't stop at the first cause, there are almost always multiple causes. Causes can be the effects of deeper causes, so keep digging through the layers!

To visualize the impact you can *mark blockers* on your task board. For instance by giving them a special color like red or a symbol that shows that a person or the whole team is blocked. This helps to make people aware of blockers and give high priority to removing blockers.

You can visualize work in progress with *work aging*: measuring the time that items of work have been in progress. This shows how long it takes to complete work and deliver. If the work age starts climbing, then maybe something is slowing you down or getting in your way. Also, work items that stand out by taking longer to complete can indicate problems. You can set a time limit and investigate all work items that go above it; just like a work in progress limit, this is something to experiment with to find out what threshold works for you.

To gather information about a problem teams can use *brainstorming*. In a brainstorming session, people generate ideas and solutions. It's not allowed to criticize ideas, you want people to think freely and bring up as many solutions as possible. When you are facilitating brainstorming to understand an existing problem, do make sure to distinguish facts from assumptions or opinions by checking what people mention during the session and asking follow-up questions. Ask questions to understand what is brought up, not to judge.

To collect and structure information, *mindmaps* are a great practice. Ask people to bring up anything they know about the problem and add that to the map. Use a large screen or projector so that everyone can see the mindmap while it's being built. Things will change often while creating the map, a good tool should support this and make it easy to move things around and restructure where needed. It's also possible to use mindmaps while being distributed, for instance with an online tool like Miro.

Fishbone diagrams can help you to identify the possible causes of a problem. Using them with predefined categories like people, process, environment, etc., helps to look at different aspects of a problem and establish an overview of what causes problems to happen.

Asking *powerful or strength-based questions* helps people to explore problems in individual or team interviews. Examples are "when did things go well and what made it possible?", "what inspires you?", or "which unique skills does your team possess?". Being positive, these powerful questions can bring out stuff that we might overlook; often people focus too much on what's going wrong and tend to forget what's working well.

Using the *Cynefin framework*, you can select a suitable approach for problem-solving. For example, if the team is dealing with a complex problem then don't expect that they can fully understand the problem by analyzing it. The Cynefin framework suggests using probe-sense-respond to do the first analysis, then based on that try something, see what happens, learn, and adjust.

Teams can use *appreciative inquiry* to envision what might be a way to improve their understanding of the problem. The main benefit of appreciative inquiry lies in the questions that we ask when we use it. These questions help to focus on what works and the things that people care about instead of looking at problems and deficiencies.

Teams can use many different *retrospective exercises* to get a better understanding of problems. Examples of retrospective exercises to analyze problems are Mad Sad Glad, 1-word Retro, 5 Times Why, constellation, and Stop the Line. My advice is to pick an exercise that suits the problem at hand and fits with the people involved in exploring it.

To understand a problem, teams can *collect data and facts* to find out what is actually happening and the impact it has. Examples of metrics are how long a work item was blocked for, how many items are blocked or impeded for similar reasons, etc. You can use questions like how frequently a problem is happening, how much time it takes, how much money we are losing, etc.

If there's no direct data available, invest time to *define mea-surements* and start measuring to get a better insight into a problem. My experience is that defining measurements already increases your insight; you'll find out what you know and don't know about a problem. Once you start measuring it, you will become better able to manage it. Also, what gets measured, gets done. If your measurement doesn't seem to help you, try a different measurement to see if that one provides useful insights.

When teams are building a shared understanding of problems using one or more of the approaches described above, they need to take sufficient time to investigate what's happening.

Know that jumping to solutions before deeply un-derstanding the problem can be costly! Teams might waste time as they are not solving the real problem. And as the problem remains, it will keep on bothering your team.

As a facilitator, you can cultivate curiosity and tolerance for discomfort to ensure we have explored problems well often before trying to solve them.

While doing root cause analysis, team members often tend to stop with two or three causes when teams do it on their own. The risk is that they do not identify the real root causes.

 It can help to have someone from outside the team to facilitate the root cause analysis. As an independent facilitator they can help teams to dig deeper into problems.

Once there is a shared understanding of the problem, the next step is to look for solutions to solve it.

Exploring Effective Solutions

To solve impediments, teams can apply existing "good practices". For example, solutions that have worked to solve similar problems, or proven solutions described using patterns.

There are many practices described and used by people all around the world, so why reinvent the wheel? I prefer to reuse what is already out there, things that I've seen working, or that I've read about and feel that I have sufficient understanding of to experiment with.

You probably need to tailor a practice for it to be effective for solving your problem in your specific circumstances.

Practices are not recipes! I prefer to view them as patterns, a way of thinking and an approach to doing something.

Some examples of practices for solving impediments are:

- Minimum Viable Product
- Definition of Ready
- Coding quality practices
- Configuration management and continuous integration
- Task board
- Managing the workflow
- DevOps
- Working agreements
- Safety checks
- Improving the way people work together

Here are some suggestions on applying these practices for solving impediments. Think of it as a toolbox, a collection of things that I've seen working for teams when they needed to solve impediments.

Solving Impediments:

If the customer's needs are unclear, create a hypothesis and deploy a *Minimum Viable Product* (MVP) to find out what your customers really want. You can use a practice like Lean Startup to learn more about your customers. My suggestion: Think about what you can deliver to get feedback and increase your understanding. With the MVP in Lean Startup, you don't have to code to have a testable product. It can also be a simple survey, paper prototype, or roleplay; anything that helps you to identify customer's needs.

If your User Stories often contain insufficient or wrong information, maybe the team can set up a *Definition of Ready* (DoR) to verify the quality of stories before taking them into consideration. The Definition of Ready can include criteria such as the INVEST principle, personas, and acceptance criteria. Don't forget that user stories are prompts for discussions. When something is unclear then my advice is to collaborate directly to solve that.

If there are problems with the quality of your code, think about *coding quality practices* like pair programming, code walkthroughs or reviews, or static code analysis to improve the quality. Use them to find and solve bugs, and also to think about how to prevent them in the future.

If your build is often broken by code changes, consider practices from *configuration management (CM) or continuous integration (CI)*. Try to automate your delivery pipeline as much as possible to get fast and reliable feedback after committing code.

If team members are having difficulties in coordinating their work, how about making the work visible on a *task board* and do daily stand-up meetings at the board to discuss what needs to be done. When you're a distributed team, you might want to use a (cloud-based) online agile tool.

If teams seem to be overloaded with work, think about practices for *managing the workflow*. Examples are limiting work in progress (WIP), sustainable pace, adding slack in your planning, theory of constraints (ToC), or setting clear goals and priorities. In your stand-up, work from right to left in your value stream to identify constraints and manage bottlenecks to get stuff delivered.

If communication and collaboration seem to be lacking between people from development and operations, maybe use *DevOps* principles and practices to create end-to-end teams with people from development and operations. Automate your build and deployment processes, make them stable and repeatable. This makes it easy to deliver fast, creates the possibility to roll back changes, and ensures that everybody has access to all relevant information.

If teams are having frequent discussions about how to arrange their work together, then they may need to establish *working agreements*. Two questions that teams can ask themselves are "what will help the team to succeed or thrive?" and "how do you want to be when things get difficult?". Good working agreements minimize friction between team members. They can prevent problems and smoothen the workflow.

There should be psychological safety in teams in terms of raising issues or concerns, otherwise problems can remain unnoticed. *Safety checks* can help you to find out if people are afraid to speak up. One way to do them is to ask people to rate how safe they feel and discuss the resulting ratings in the team.

If there seem to be collaboration problems in teams, invest time in *improving the way people work together*. You can consider pairing or swapping roles between people. Arrange activities for people to get to know each other, and invite people to participate in sessions to find out what's happening and what others are doing.

As mentioned, these are just some examples of how you can use well-defined practices to solve problems. There are many more practices out there and there's a wealth of experiences on how to apply them.

 Personally, I prefer to use practices that match with agile and lean principles, as I have seen such practices to be very effective in solving problems. If teams truly adopt such practices they also reduce the chance that the same problem will happen again. I call it sustainable improvement.

When you need to decide upon a practice, you might not know if it will help you to solve the problem. What can help is to consider it as an experiment: try it out to see the result. If it works, great! If not, think about something else.

You can use a solution-focused approach to find effective solutions for dealing with impediments. For instance, by asking people to think about times when the problem that they are trying to solve wasn't there or had been less of a problem. And then follow up by asking them what they were doing at that time that was helpful and made it that way.

 Instead of coming up with something new and scary, a solution-focused approach helps people to solve a problem by doing more of the things that they are doing and hence know how to do.

There are always more solutions possible to solve the problem. Each solution has advantages and disadvantages.

To test if you have really understood the problem before applying a solution, there's my rule of three, which is based on Jerry Weinberg's rule of three from his book The Secrets of Consulting:

If you can't come up with at least three different solutions that might work to solve a problem, then you don't really understand the problem.

Here's an example of how I have used the rule of three.

A problem that many teams have is that their product owner or other stakeholders are very busy. One solution that I've seen work is to limit reporting and instead encourage people to join the product review (from push to pull). Another solution is to split your refinement sessions into two parts: One with and one without the product owner. Even better is to prepare your meetings with the product owner to get them involved and make it easier to come to decisions.

As mentioned before, don't treat practices as recipes. There are no standard solutions, "no best practices, only good practices in context" as Larry Maccherone stated (more on this in my InfoQ interview with Larry Maccherone and Jim McCurley about Quantifying the Impact of Agile Software Development Practices).

It depends on the situation what practice can be suitable to deal with an impediment.

Most of the time you will need to adapt a practice to the situation at hand for applying it effectively.

Some of the techniques to deploy practices in an effective way are:

- Devil's or angel's advocate game
- Safe-to-fail experiment
- Asking why
- Support people on an as-needed base
- Experiment
- Listen
- Checklists

Here are some examples of how I deployed these practices to solve impediments.

Deploy Practices:

I play a *devil's or angel's advocate game* to challenge how to apply a practice in a given context. Both are great ways to improve on ideas using the feedback given by the advocates.

Defining a *safe-to-fail experiment* helps to try out a practice and set yourself up for learning. It uses the probe-sense-respond approach from Cynefin for complex problems to try out new things and discover what happens.

I prefer why over how. You can do it by *asking why* to understand the needs before deploying a practice. This is also a great way to get people engaged. If they see why something is needed the chance that they support it goes up.

For me, it works to give people space to try a practice; don't enforce things but be available is what I often do. Sometimes it's best to do nothing when people are changing their way of working and *support people on an as-needed base*. Don't impose, it's pull over push to get lasting change.

You can agree that, instead of everybody adopting something new, some of the team members will *experiment* by trying out a practice or to use a practice on a subset of the cases to see how it works out. This can make it easier to see the improvement, and based on that decide to continue, adjust, or abandon.

I coach people by suggesting them to *listen* and try to understand people's concerns. Based on that, they can help them come up with one or more practices that might be useful. Leave it up to the people themselves and trust them to decide what to do and how to do it.

You can use *checklists* to tailor a practice. Checklists can help to decide on what to include or not include, how to apply a practice, etc.

There are many more techniques for applying practices, these are just some ideas to get you started. The best way to learn new practices is by doing it :-).

Deciding on the Actions

After teams have come up with several solutions to deal with an impediment, the next step is to decide which actions they will do to solve it.

Let's dive into who decides to take action and explore different approaches that agile teams can use to decide upon how to take action.

Since agile values teams and team working, preferably the team members should decide on the actions that will be done. Not a team leader, project manager, or line manager. Also not the team's product owner or Scrum master alone.

It can be the whole team, or one or more team members, depending on the impact of the decision and how much team members need to buy-in to get the actions done by the team.

 It's usually best to involve all team members in decisions on what action to take!

My advice is to at all times avoid that the team leader or Scrum master decides alone on what to do. Chances are high that team members will not buy-in and support the actions.

 I've seen teams where the Scrum master decided that "the team should communicate better". Not much would change, because nobody except the Scrum master knew what better looks like.

A practical approach to getting the team to decide on taking action is to raise the need for a decision during a time when the team is together, for instance at the daily stand-up or in a retrospective meeting.

Don't wait until a retrospective meeting to raise problems and make improvements.

The whole team is present on such occasions which makes reaching an agreement easier. This ensures that the decision is supported by all team members and that they will take action.

Many people think that consensus is the best (and only) way that teams should decide. But as often, there is no single best way.

It would be great if teams can reach consensus, but that doesn't make it the only solution. Alternatively, teams can take a decision based upon consent or agree that a working group of team members will decide.

Deciding by consent implies that, if there is no major objection to a decision by any team member, then the decision is accepted.

Deciding by consent can help you to make the best possible decision under given conditions. Also, you can get a decision made without hours of debate!

A practical and quick way that I use a lot to reach a consent decision is thumb voting or Roman voting. It's important that everyone reveals their vote at the same time, not being influenced by what others are voting. Thumb up means that a person agrees, thumb sideways means that they go along with whatever the team decides, and thumb down means that they disagree. If nobody disagrees and most members of the team support the decision with a thumb up, you can safely assume that the whole team supports the decision.

Alternatively, I suggest using the fist of five technique to come to a decision. I use it to check-in with people on a topic, if there are several low scores then we probably need to do some more work before you can reach a decision. I then ask people why they score low, what their objections are, and what we can do to raise their score.

The consent principle is often used in organizations that are applying sociocracy or sociocracy 3.0.

Sociocracy 3.0 calls this way of deciding and experimenting "good enough for now, safe enough to try".

You can accelerate decisions by limiting the time for getting to a decision with a timebox. Make it clear up front how much time people will get before a decision has to be made. People shouldn't feel overly pressured, there should be enough time to have everyone involved in the decision.

If you're still unable to decide at the end of the timebox, you can agree to pick one possible solution and give it a try and experiment. Agree on the expected outcome and set a time when you will check if the outcome has been met.

Sometimes it needs further investigation before a decision to take action can be made. In such cases, teams can decide to establish a working group of one or more team members. This group explores the viability and consequences of specific actions before deciding.

The team can agree to leave the final decision to the working group, or ask the working group to report back and then decide as a team.

Explicit and clear decisions to take action help agile teams to effectively deal with impediments. To make sure that the actions will be done by the team they need to choose how the team decides.

A question I often get is who should be handling and solving impediments? Should it be the Scrum master? Their agile coach? Or the team itself?

As it is the team that decides to take action, it's also up to the team members to do the actions. This is vital, without the actions the impediments remain and will continue to hamper the team.

 Team members can recognize and solve impediments themselves. For most of them, they don't need a Scrum master or coach. If they see a problem, I expect team members to take action and solve it.

Some of the main reasons to involve team members when dealing with impediments are:

- Team members other than the Scrum master or tech lead might be better qualified to solve an impediment.
- Problems are often too complex for one person to solve them.
- Viewing an impediment from different angles helps to find effective solutions.
- Many problems have to do with the way how people work together. By definition, one person alone cannot solve such a problem.
- You can expect from team members that they are able to organize their work, which includes dealing with problems.
- Teams should not depend on a single person to get problems out of the way.

I interviewed William Perry on his book Teams, what's in it for me? where we discussed what causes unfinished actions:

The excuse that is often made by team members for unfinished work is that they have insufficient time to do things. But this is almost never the real reason. In practice, it often turns out that team members are unsure of what is really needed, or don't know how to do it.

As a Scrum master, team leader, or agile coach, you can help people in finding ways to do their actions. Also, you can create an environment where people feel safe enough to try something out.

 A team that I worked in was looking for ways to improve code quality. We decided to try-out static code analysis, where several team members used different tools to explore code they'd written themselves. Once we got more familiar with it, we paired up to demonstrate the different tools inspecting random code modules. There wasn't any pressure on the team, in fact, they got time and budget to explore this and come up with a proposal.

Recognizing impediments, understanding how they hinder teams, exploring effective solutions, and deciding how to solve and who takes action; these are the four steps described in this chapter to deal effectively with impediments in teams. You can practice these steps to develop problem-solving skills in your teams.

Intermezzo: Agile Frameworks and Methods

An agile way of working implies handling impediments as soon as they become visible and dealing with them to enable teams to deliver. There are many agile frameworks and methods that provide guidance on handling impediments.

Scrum suggests that teams should identify and remove impediments. But handling impediments isn't a thing that you should only do when working with Scrum. If you use SAFe, LeSS, Scrum@scale, Kanban, Nexus, Lean, or any other agile framework or approach, or a combination of these, then impediments and how you deal with them will matter too.

Let's explore what agile methods and frameworks have to say about impediments and what solutions they provide us to deal with impediments.

Scrum

The focus of Scrum when it comes to problem-solving is on impediments that teams face. According to Scrum, an impediment is anything that keeps the team from getting work done and that slows them down.

The 2017 Scrum guide states that daily Scrums "identify impediments to development for removal". One of the three suggested questions for the daily Scrum in the guide is for team members to raise impediments that prevent them or the development team from meeting the sprint goal.

Where Scrum expects team members to raise impediments, in practice, it isn't always clear if there's a problem or what the impact will be. I suggest bringing up any potential problem and briefly discuss them, and decide how to deal with them either on the spot or allocate additional time (preferably directly after the daily Scrum or on the same day) to do a detailed analysis and decide what to do.

According to Scrum, daily Scrums are about identifying impediments, not removal.

I agree that you should focus on identifying impediments in the daily Scrum. But if the team can find solutions and agree what to do at that moment, why not seize the opportunity? Make sure to limit the time spent on solving the problem in the daily Scrum. If you somehow sense that it needs more time then park the problem and solve it outside the daily Scrum.

The Scrum guide states that the Scrum master serves the team by removing impediments to the development's team progress. I've seen this interpreted as the Scrum master being responsible for "impediment hunting". I've also seen people say that the Scrum master is responsible for solving all impediments.

My opinion is that Scrum masters shouldn't be the one removing all impediments. Team members themselves should solve problems, instead of having their Scrum master do it for them. This enables self-organization throughout the whole team. Team members can reach out to the Scrum master for help, but they shouldn't depend on the Scrum master for solving impediments.

Where the Scrum guide does mention that impediments should be raised and dealt with, it doesn't provide guidance on how to explore, understand, or solve impediments. The guide leaves it over to the team to decide what to do and how to do it.

The Scrum guide suggests that the development team discusses in the sprint review what went well during the sprint, what problems it ran into, and how those problems were solved.

I strongly argue against discussing team problems in the sprint review. Product reviews are there for teams to get feedback, not to report. Information should be transparent and accessible at all times. You don't need meetings to share information, discussing team issues in the sprint review sounds like the team reporting on what they will bring up in their retrospective!

Retrospectives can be used to explore and solve impediments. Make it a separate meeting to inspect and adapt, don't put it on the agenda of the product review.

 You can do retrospectives at the project level, or after every main delivery, or just after a couple of sprints, where representatives from teams meet with stakeholders from the project, business, etc.

Scaled Agile Framework

The Scaled Agile Framework (SAFe) suggests that managers should eliminate impediments. They should also support teams by helping them remove systemic impediments and implementing continuous improvement backlog items (as described in The Evolving Role of Managers in Lean-Agile Development).

SAFe also expects Scrum masters to support the elimination of impediments and address blocking issues that go beyond the team's authority or require support from other teams:

> Many blocking issues will be beyond the team's authority or may require support from other teams. The Scrum Master supports the team in addressing and eliminating these issues to improve the likelihood of achieving the objectives of the Iteration. © Scaled Agile, Inc.

Where I can relate to this, I have two concerns about managers and Scrum masters dealing with impediments:

 Supporting teams in solving systemic impediments can be helpful, as long as teams remain in the lead about what to solve when and how to solve it. It should not hamper the capability of teams to be self-organized.

 For eliminating impediments, I strongly suggest that managers and Scrum masters collaborate with team members while doing this. The reason for this is to assure that what they do makes it easier for teams to do their work, not harder. This also supports that teams learn how to solve problems themselves instead of depending on other people to do it for them.

According to SAFe, release train engineers should escalate and track impediments.

The term "escalate" can be read as reporting the problem and leaving it up to other people to decide what to do. This approach hampers self-organization. My advice is to only use it as a last resort. Preferably people should collaboratively solve problems and keep in close contact during the whole process. Treat solving problems as a shared responsibility.

SAFe suggests that stakeholders join the inspect and adapt event. This event, held at the end of a program increment, includes a retrospective and a problem-solving workshop where teams reflect and identify improvement backlog items.

For systemic problems, SAFe proposes using root cause analysis to address the actual causes rather than symptoms.

Root cause analysis can be used to get a shared understanding of problems, which makes it easier to collaboratively solve them.

Large Scale-Scrum

Large Scale-Scrum (LeSS) aims to apply Scrum in a large-scale context, as simply as possible.

This is how LeSS suggest that a LeSS Scrum Master should work with teams in dealing with impediments:

> A LeSS Scrum Master will encounter complex large-scale problems and she'll need to resist resolving them with complex large-scale solutions. Instead, she'll need to leverage the spirit of Scrum and find simple ways to empower people to resolve their impediments. This approach leads to large-scale, yet simple, solutions.

Large Scale-Scrum proposes to do overall retrospectives to explore systemic and organizational issues above the level of a single team. In such a retrospective, the product owner, Scrum masters, team representatives, and managers, discuss cross-team, organizational, and systemic problems within the organization.

Retrospectives can be very effective for analyzing and solving problems, provided that they are well facilitated and that all participants feel safe enough to speak up.

Team coaches in LeSS focus on making organizational impediments visible. This makes solving impediments by those involved easier.

LeSS suggests applying Lean thinking to address impediments to the flow of value. It also proposes inspiring people to continuously strive to improve that flow.

Scrum@Scale

Scrum@Scale applies impediment removal at scale to increase the speed of the entire organization. Product owner teams prioritize impediments in the backlog to have them resolved. The Scrum of Scrums Master prioritizes impediments and is responsible for removing impediments that the team cannot address themselves.

Preferably product owner teams should work together with the teams when they prioritize impediments, to assure that impact of impediments on the teams is taken into account.

The Scrum@Scale guide describes how to deal with impediments in a Scrum of Scrums:

> The Scrum of Scrums Master should facilitate the refinement of an impediment backlog wherein impediments are identified as "ready" and prioritized to be removed. The teams then determine how best to remove them and how they will know when they are "done." In some cases, impediment resolution may require product development, in which case, involvement from the Scrum of Scrums Chief Product Owner and Product Owner Team will be necessary.

The executive action team coordinates multiple Scrum of Scrums and interfaces with non-agile parts of the organization. They are the final stop for impediments that the Scrum of Scrums cannot remove.

 Raising impediments to the level where they can be dealt with effectively make sense. Not all impediments need to be raised. Allow teams to solve those that they can solve themselves. Teams can also work together to solve an impediment, supported (but not directed) by managers.

Continuous improvement and impediment removal work closely together in Scrum@scale to identify problems and make them visible, create an environment to prioritize and remove impediments, and verify the resulting improvements.

Nexus

Nexus is a framework for developing and sustaining scaled product and software delivery initiatives. It has been developed by Ken Schwaber and Scrum.org.

The Nexus™ Guide mentions dependencies between teams, these can be seen as impediments at scale. They call out three main dependencies; requirements, domain knowledge, and software and test artifacts. Teams can reduce the number of dependencies between them by mapping requirements, knowledge, and artifacts to the same team.

 This kind of mapping fosters end-to-end responsibility and increases the autonomy of teams. It also reduces the change that impediments span across multiple teams, making it easier for teams to recognize and solve them.

The Nexus integration team plays a central role when it comes to impediments. The integration team should ensure that there is an integrated increment at least once per sprint.

> Integration includes resolving any technical and non-technical cross-team constraints that may impede a Nexus' ability to deliver a constantly Integrated Increment.

The integration team acts as a focal point for integration; the role is more about coaching, highlighting awareness of dependencies and cross-team issues for teams to resolve themselves.

The work to resolve issues affecting many teams has priority in Nexus. To ensure this, Nexus proposes that members of the Nexus Integration Team are also members of the individual Scrum teams.

Members from different teams can bring up impediments that go beyond their team during the Nexus Daily Scrum. Next, they can collaborate to find solutions and agree on what will be done. The individual Scrum teams take back issues to their individual Scrum teams for planning inside their individual daily Scrum events

 Bring up impediments as soon as possible. If many impediments become visible late in a sprint, then you may want to investigate what causes them to remain invisible for so long.

The Nexus™ Guide describes how to do continuous improvement. In the Nexus sprint retrospective, appropriate representatives from across a Nexus identify issues that have impacted more than a single team. Teams can then discuss these issues in their own retrospective and agree upon actions. Finally, appropriate representatives from the Scrum Teams meet again and agree on how to visualize and track the identified actions, allowing the Nexus as a whole to adapt.

Other Methods and Frameworks

Kanban draws upon the Theory of Constraints (ToC) to look for the biggest constraint on the system as a whole. Such constraints are very similar to impediments. ToC suggests focusing improvement efforts on that single constraint. After removing this constraint, then find out what is now the biggest constraint.

Lean defines the concept of waste as activities that do not directly add value as perceived by the customer. We can explore waste to find the impediments that are causing it. Being aware of the waste caused by impediments encourages people to deal with them.

During a Scrum of Scrums or Scaled Daily Scrum, impediments that hamper collaboration between teams can become visible. Members from different teams can decide to work together to address such impediments.

Handling Impediments Beyond the Team Level

Many impediments are things that teams can deal with themselves. Being self-organized, teams can come up with solutions and solve the impediments that they face within the team.

But chances are that teams will uncover impediments that go beyond their influence or span of control. As an example, think about systemic organizational issues, or problems that hinder multiple teams or need management support to solve them.

Some of the challenges that teams face in dealing with such impediments are:

- It's hard to oversee impediments only looking from a team perspective.
- Teams may have limited information about problems, not all information may be available or accessible to them.
- Problems can involve many stakeholders, where it's often hard for teams to get them all together to align their views and decide what to do.
- Actions needed to deal with the impediment may be outside the team's control or influence.

The nature of these kinds of problems makes it very difficult to impossible for teams to solve them on their own. We need to go up higher in the organization to properly address such impediments.

In this chapter, I'll explore how we can handle impediments beyond the team level.

Systemic Impediments

Preferably problems are addressed at the lowest possible level. This is usually the cheapest and fastest way to do it. For many problems, this is the team level as I explored in the chapter dealing with impediments in teams.

But what if the problems that we are facing seem to go beyond the team level? Then we need a different approach.

Examples of impediments that can go beyond the team level are:

- Organizational procedures or processes
- Lack of people or skills in teams
- Limited budgets for products, projects, or teams
- Organizational structure, barriers between different groups
- Cultural or political issues
- Conflicting goals in the organization

These kinds of impediments relate to the "system" in which teams are doing their work, the context in which they have to operate.

In this book I will call impediments that go beyond the team level *systemic impediments*.

Systemic impediments are likely to impact multiple teams. They may also impact the relationship between teams and their stakeholders.

It's preferred that people from different teams and other parts of the organization work together to solve systemic impediments.

Traditionally it has been managers in organizations that took care of these kinds of systemic problems. With more and more organizations adopting agile ways of working, this is changing. In an agile organization, agile teams will solve most of the impediments themselves.

 Self-organizing agile teams prefer to take action themselves. They do not rely on managers telling them what to do or how to do their work.

Managers can work together with teams to resolve impediments that teams raise. In the book Create Your Successful Agile Project, Johanna Rothman suggests that managers focus on the flow of value and think about how they can be of help to their teams:

> Great managers start with this question: "What do I need to do to see a flow of value from this team?" If the manager optimizes for value flow, the manager will see what his or her role could be.

The few impediments left where managers have to be involved to solve them are the hard ones. They often have to do with organizational barriers or company goals or culture. Managers should focus on getting these issues solved with the help of teams, where teams will solve most of the other issues themselves.

Such an approach will free up time for managers to look further into the future. What's going to be the next thing in three months or a year? What challenges or possible problems could that bring? How can we prepare for that? Managers can now work on strategic problem-solving and preventing problems, leaving operational problem-solving to the teams.

Collaboration is still key. Even though there's a different focus in teams and management when it comes to problem-solving, they should stay in close contact and reach out frequently to work together and stay involved with each other's activities.

Systemic impediments that are too tough for teams to resolve themselves might not reach the levels above the team needed to solve them. For instance, if teams don't have access to management levels above their own manager, where their manager decides to not raise their issues.

In large organizations, teams can be limited in various ways when it comes to addressing impediments. Examples are:

- The way the organization is structured into departments, teams, etc
- Politics and the power distribution
- The culture, open and transparent or blaming culture
- Information sharing, knowledge is power

Conway's law comes to mind when we think about how the organizational structure impacts the architecture of the systems that they develop. The organizational structure has a similar impact on the capabilities to handle impediments. Where there are barriers between different parts of the organization, it becomes harder to solve problems.

When organizations structure into product-based end-to-end teams this often increases their capabilities to handle impediments effectively.

In some organizations, managers seem to feel people should just get things done despite the impediments, i.e., without really addressing them. The managers focus on getting things done where they accept that impediments are a necessary part of how things work. This kind of thinking makes it difficult for teams to invest time in understanding impediments.

 Prevent impediments from becoming accepted as the norm. True agile teams have zero tolerance for impediments and they focus on continuous improvement for the future, not just on getting things done now.

Handling Systemic Impediments

The steps for dealing with systemic impediments are:

- Recognizing systemic impediments
- Understanding the impact impediments have
- Exploring effective solutions to systemic impediments
- Deciding on organizational-wide actions

Given the complexity of systemic impediments, I suggest allocating enough time to perform the steps mentioned above.

It makes sense to devote plenty of time to recognizing and understanding the impediments. A good shared understanding of impediments often makes it easier and cheaper to come up with solutions and get actions done.

Solving systemic problems is not technical work, it has to do with people working together.

It is key to establish a collaborative culture during the whole process of spotting and analyzing impediments, and coming up with solutions and deciding on the answers. If needed, make sure that there's an independent facilitator who can guide the people involved through the process steps.

Recognizing Systemic Impediments

The first step in dealing with systemic impediments beyond the team level is to recognize them. Where the approaches used to spot systemic impediments are similar to spotting team impediments, it can be harder to understand systemic impediments.

Some of the things that make it more difficult to understand systemic impediments are:

- Systemic impediments are complex problems without a clear cause-effect relationship.
- The people involved in a systemic problem are part of the system that causes it to happen.
- Systemic problems are often unpredictable, it's hard to find out why something is happening.
- Investigating a systemic problem can impact the problem or the effects of it.
- It's usually impossible to get a complete view of the situation and the systemic problem at hand.
- People can be biased and have blind spots.

It may help to put in extra effort to uncover systemic impediments.

 To be able to recognize systemic impediments, make time to stop and reflect, and look for patterns.

It's important to distinguish between team and organizational impediments early on when recognizing them. Where the team themselves can solve the first, the second ones need to be coordinated or escalated beyond the team.

The fly high technique described in the guest blog making retrospectives interesting can be used to make this distinction and help teams decide to either work consciously to solve them or to reach out for help.

Activities to recognize and visualize systemic impediments are:

- Scrum of Scrums
- Product reviews
- Agile retrospectives
- Blameless Post-mortems
- Pre-mortems
- Impediment boards
- Stop the Line
- Process assessments
- Self-assessments
- Surveys

Let me give some examples of how you can use these activities.

Recognize Systemic Impediments:

In *Scrum of Scrums* teams work to coordinate their work toward a shared delivery. During a Scrum of Scrums, attendees can bring up impediments. Members from different teams can discuss the impediments and explore what impact it has on their team and for deliveries.

The main purpose of *product reviews* is to demonstrate the product and get feedback. During the review, discussions may arise that signal problems. It can, for instance, be in the way that people react to the presentations, communicate with each other, or the kind of issues that they bring up.

Agile retrospectives are mainly used to reflect how things are going and to decide upon improvement actions. Where most retrospectives are done at the team level, it also possible to do them at the project or product level, or to involve people from different parts of product development or the organization in the team's retrospective.

Blameless post-mortems are somewhat similar to retrospectives. You can use them to explore problems that have happened to learn from them and decide upon actions to prevent similar problems in the future. The term blameless makes clear that there should be no blaming in a post mortem, as that inhibits effective participation and impacts the effect of the meeting.

In *pre-mortems*, attendees imagine that something has failed to work backward to determine what may have caused the failure. Based on this understanding they can take actions to prevent problems from happening. Pre-mortems should foster a positive discussion on problems, making it possible to visualize situations before they have happened.

Teams can use *impediment boards* to visualize problems that require the attention or help from their managers. It can be a board in an obeya room or a specific section on the team board where teams invite managers to discuss impediments and collaboratively work on solutions. Make sure that these boards are visited frequently to solve problems as quickly as possible.

People should be encouraged to bring up problems as soon as possible to handle them when the impact is still limited. One way to do this is to *stop the line* when there's a problem. Stop the line is commonly used in lean manufacturing to deal with impediments and ensure quality.

You can do *process assessments* to explore how people do their work and compare that to documented processes. It can be processes prescribed by the organization, or those that come from maturity or capability models, industry's good practices, or formal standards or frameworks.

Traditionally assessments are done by experts external to the team or organization. With agile we see a trend toward *self-assessments*. Teams do these assessments themselves, supported (where needed) by coaches or consultants. By engaging people into the assessment they will be more willing to accept the outcome and take action.

You can use *surveys* to collect information about how your products or services are being perceived. Where numeric data from surveys can signal problems, open questions can provide insights into the problems. Examples of such surveys are Net Promotor Score (NPS),

Recognizing systemic impediments isn't always easy. The above practices can help you; here's some additional guidance on how to apply these practices.

In the product review, the development team can discuss what went well during the sprint, what problems it ran into, and how they solved those problems. These discussions can provide insight into impediments and lead to decisions about addressing them.

The facilitator of the product review should keep an eye out for signals and handle them properly, for instance by taking notes so that they are followed up after the review.

Agile retrospectives are a great way to solve impediments and continuously improve the way of working. Depending on the problem, use a set of suitable retrospective exercises in the retrospective meeting to increase understanding of impediments and decide upon actions.

There needs to be psychological safety in retrospectives. Retrospective facilitators should address any blaming promptly to enable that people will feel safe enough to bring up problems.

One time in a meeting that I attended I saw how the architect took over when the group was discussing a problem and started blaming people. Everybody became silent and the meeting stalled. The architect, becoming aware of what he had caused, decided to leave the meeting. Next, the meeting facilitator managed to get the meeting back into shape, where the group decided upon the actions without the architect being present.

Stop the line originates from Toyota where Taiichi Ohno introduced the andon cord and authorized every employee on the assembly line to immediately pull the andon cord when they see a problem or discover a defect.

When someone sees a problem they should inform all affected and work together to solve it.

After the andon cord has been pulled, people come together to analyze the problem and find out what is causing it. After the root causes have been identified and removed, work continues.

Organizations can use process assessments to verify if people follow the defined processes. The outcomes from process assessments can be used to define improvement actions.

The biggest challenges that I see with process assessments are establishing buy-in and getting improvement actions done. You have to involve people in the assessment to get acceptance of the results. The assessment team should not impose actions, people should define their own improvement actions.

Self-assessments engage people. They are more willing to take action as they have a better understanding of why they need to do the improvement actions and what benefits they will get from doing the improvements.

 Teams can self-assess their agility with the Agile Self-assessment Game. They play the Agile Self-assessment Game to reflect on how things are going and agree on the next steps in their agile journey.

You can recognize and visualize systemic impediments using the activities described in this section. Once there is a shared view of the impediment, then you can take the next step.

Understanding the Impact Impediments Have

The second step in dealing with systemic impediments is analyzing them to understand the impact that they have on the organization.

 Use information from recognizing and visualizing the impediment (the first step) as a starting point for further analysis.

Impediments can impact teams and organizations in several ways:

- Impediments might block one or more teams.
- Impediments may slow down people from different teams.
- It can be difficult for teams and stakeholders to work together to get things done due to impediments.
- Impediments can make it harder for people to do their work.
- There can be additional work that needs to be done due to impediments.
- Impediments may impact plans or commitments regarding delivery dates, costs, etc.

Systemic impediments often impact multiple teams. The impact might however differ from team to team.

 Analysis of impediments should be deep enough to show the impact for each team and the stakeholders and customers.

When an impediment has only limited impact then it might not be worth solving it. There's always a cost-benefit aspect that you need to consider, comparing the impact of an impediment with the investment needed to solve them.

 The impact of impediments are often significant. It's not only the waste of time and money, but it also includes losses due to the cost of delay in delivering the product, frustrated team members, credibility loss from your stakeholders, reputation of your brand, etc.

Bigger impediments can be broken down into smaller parts to be able to deal with them. This requires strong communication and collaboration skills.

 Where impediments are big, an approach that often works is to pull out one major aspect of an impediment and work on that to get some first results.

There are several possible approaches for analyzing the impact of systemic impediments:

- Value stream mapping
- Process flow diagrams
- Root cause analysis
- Portfolio Kanban board
- Quantify the impact
- Systems thinking
- Force field analysis
- Cluster blockers and defects
- Impediment impact diagrams

Here are my suggestions for applying these approaches.

Analyzing Impact:

Value stream mapping provides insight into the end-to-end product delivery flow. The diagrams help to visualize impediments and show how much waste they cause. You can also analyze bottlenecks and wait times and find ways to improve delivery time. To increase throughput and flow you can remove major impediments going right to left in the value flow. Our book Getting Value out of Agile Retrospectives explains how to use value stream mapping in retrospectives.

Process flow diagrams visualize processes with their input and output. They give insight into the connections between processes. They are more detailed than value stream maps, hence proving more information about the impact when one or more processes have become an impediment to delivery.

With *root cause analysis* you can determine the first or "root" causes of a problem. Draw a cause-effect diagram by repeatedly asking why, until you have reached the root causes. Note that there are usually multiple causes, so don't stop when you found the first one. Addressing the root causes will prevent similar problems from happening in the future.

A Portfolio Kanban board can visualize how work flows and find anything that impedes the flow across the value chain. It can help you focus on the flow from conception between teams to when it is in the customer's hand. You can use techniques in a similar way as work in progress, lead time, and work aging: to explore problems with work that crosses the boundaries of different teams, or visualize impediments to the workflow at a more coarse level i.e. feature/epic/project.

The impact that impediments have is often underestimated. When you think that that might be the case, I suggest to *quantify the impact*, for instance by estimating how much time or money is wasted or how much they delay delivery.

For measuring the impact on team motivation and morale you may want to count the number of "wtf" (how often people say "what the fuck" or something similar when they stumble on a problem or feel surprised by something) or use a happiness index (as described in my book Getting Value out of Agile Retrospectives).

Being systemic problems, a *systems thinking* approach can be a suitable way to deal with them. It helps to develop a holistic view of the problem and explore the relationships within the system. Systemic impediments often have a major impact on these relationships; using a systems thinking approach helps you to learn more about impediments and become able to better address them.

Force field analysis can be used to explore the forces that keep the situation the same and forces that are pushing the situation to change. Insight in these forces helps to better understand why problems exist and what to influence when you want to solve problems. It's an effective technique that explores the context of problems.

You can *cluster blockers and defects* to understand systemic impediments. In the InfoQ article using blocker clustering, defect clustering, and prioritization for process improvement Klaus Leopold and Troy Magennis show how to use information from your Kanban board to find the impediments with the biggest impact.

Impediment impact diagrams is a technique developed by Ken Power which is described in the paper Understanding the impact of impediments in agile teams and organizations. It uses a matrix consisting of impact and influence to identify high-impact impediments that teams can solve themselves or that they need help with.

Once there a good insight into the impact of an impediment, then you're ready to take the next step where you explore solutions.

Exploring Effective Solutions to Systemic Impediments

Finding solutions to solve systemic impediments can be hard. Knowing up front if these solutions will be effective is even harder. We're dealing with complex adaptive systems where you can't predict what the impact of a change will be. You need to think carefully about the effect that making a change may have elsewhere on the overall system.

Cynefin suggests to use a probe-sense-respond approach: Try a solution, see how that works out, and adapt the solution based on the feedback that we get.

Some of the practices for solving systemic impediments are:

- Collaborative problem solving
- Self-selection
- Co-creation
- Futurespectives
- Solution-focused
- Emergent practice
- LEGO® Serious Play

Let's explore the possibilities to apply these practices.

Solving Systemic Impediments:
Collaborative problem solving approaches involve large groups of people to come up with solutions and decide on the way forward. Examples are Community-Powered Problem Solving and practices like 1-2-4-all and Appreciative Interviews from Liberating Structures. The biggest benefits are the

diversity of the group which leads to better solutions, and the way people are engaged which increases acceptance of the solutions.

You can use *self-selection* to solve organization problems around structuring teams. The book Creating Great Teams - How Self-Selection Lets People Excel describes how to facilitate people self-organizing into small, cross-functional teams. The strength of this approach is that it allows people to decide what they want to work on and with whom. It builds a strong foundation for establishing high-performing autonomous teams who will be able to better deal with impediments.

Co-creation is a collaborative approach for coming up with solutions, where you involve stakeholders, customers, and other people who have a stake in the outcome. Applying co-creation for solving impediments can help you to find sustainable solutions that are closely aligned to your customer's needs; solutions that solve their (and your) problems.

A *futurespective* is a technique where you break free from your current situation and limitations to find innovative solutions. It starts by placing yourself in the future and imagining that your problem are solved. Together you explore how this looks and works, you can even celebrate this success. Next, you discuss how you got here: What enabled you to solve the problem, what made the difference? Going back to the present, you decide upon the first steps that will help you to deal effectively with the problem at hand. Futurespectives are somewhat similar to pre-mortems, the difference is that in a pre-mortem you imagine that the team has failed where in the futerespective it has succeeded.

A *solution-focused* approach works by finding out what works and amplifying that to solve problems. It's about getting better by doing more of the things that you are already doing and which you are good at. You can apply solution focused in a strengths-based retrospective.

Instead of trying to install a perfect solution using a best practice, *emergent practice* is an approach where you adapt a solution along the way to solve an impediment. Emerge means that we don't know the solution upfront, it actually emerges when we are solving the problem. Thinking in emergent practices can scale as we experiment with practices and apply our learnings to widen their usage.

With *LEGO® Serious Play* people can build 3D models that mirror situations. It's a technique that improves group problem solving using metaphors and storytelling. Building and discussing these models help people to create alignment and purpose, and to explore possible solutions to the problems that are being faced or that might happen.

Note that some of the practices from Understanding the Impact Impediments Have can also be used to explore effective solutions.

Applying a combination of the above approaches will give you a variety of solutions. Such diversity increases the chance of effectively solving your impediments.

Deciding on Organizational-wide Actions

Now that solutions to solving impediments are known, it's time to decide how to take action. The main decisions to be made are: what to do, when to do it, and who should take action.

People who have been involved in the decision are more likely to take action.

 Organizations can apply collaborative decision-making techniques to engage people into the decision and increase the chance that actions are actually implemented and followed up by them.

Activities that can be used to decide upon organizational-wide actions are:

- Obeya room
- Consent decision making
- Hypothesis
- Fact-based decision making
- Impact estimation tables

Let's explore how we can apply these practices.

Deciding on actions:

The main purpose of an *Obeya room* is to have a place where you can make information visible so that all involved can discuss it and decide what to do. The concept originates from lean to support visual management and enable teamwork. I've seen organizations that setup obeya rooms to manage their agile transformation. Impediments are brought up by anyone and lifted up toward the organizational level where they most likely can be solved. After deciding on the actions they are tracked to completion.

Consent decision making is an effective approach for making group decisions. Decisions are made in the absence of objections, which makes it possible to decide faster while keeping people involved. The group works on crafting the actions until the point is reached where none of the participants has paramount objections, then the decision is ratified. Sociocracy 3.0 suggests using consent decision making by calling it "good enough for now, safe enough to try".

You can use a *hypothesis* to state the possible outcome of actions, which supports making decisions about which solutions to apply and how to apply them successfully. The hypothesis should be unambiguous and testable, making it possible to verify if the impediment was solved by taking the actions. Using a hypothesis supports organizational learning and leads to improved action-taking.

Fact-based decision making implies making decisions based on figures, data, and evidence. You can use it to remove uncertainty when deciding which actions to take to solve impediments. Apply it iteratively by collecting data and collaboratively analyzing the impact of possible solutions and deliberating the pros and cons until you feel confident enough to decide on the actions.

With *Impact estimation tables* you analyze solutions to make a decision. They are described in the book Value Planning by Tom Gilb. According to Gilb, the purpose of impact estimation tables is to force us to think clearly, and to reason logically, about our selection of means for reaching our clear objectives. Quantifying the impact of solutions helps to better decide what solutions to pick.

After a decision is made, you execute actions to solve impediments.

Dealing with Organizational-wide Impediments

Recognizing systemic impediments, understanding their impact, exploring effective solutions, and deciding on organizational-wide actions; these are the four steps described in this chapter to deal effectively with organizational-wide impediments. You can practice these steps to develop problem-solving skills throughout your organization.

When working on organizational-wide impediments, there's always a balance to be found between one solution that fits all or multiple solutions that suit the different needs of teams or stakeholders.

 If it turns out that an impediment is only impacting one or a few teams, then those involved should be able to solve it themselves in a way that works best for them. Don't impose a generic solution, instead give them space and support them in exploring their own solutions.

Of course, it's ok if members from other teams offer their help. But the teams that are being impacted should not be depending on other teams to solve impediments.

Collaboration is key for solving organizational-wide impediments. Always make sure to involve everyone who has a stake in solving the impediment or who is impacted by the actions.

Increasing your Problem-solving Effectiveness

Although the steps described in previous chapters on dealing with impediments sound rather straightforward and easy, solving impediments is often perceived as stressful and difficult by many people. It often means changing something and trying things that you haven't done before.

To recap: Agile teams need to be able to handle impediments effectively. Let's explore examples of the difficulties that I see that people have when dealing with impediments, and look at solutions that will make it easier to handle impediments and solve problems.

This chapter explores what you can do to become more effective in dealing with impediments, turning it into a practice and habit that supports continuous improvement.

Understand What You Are Trying to Solve

When working with people, I often see them acting on symptoms and taking actions before they really understand the problem. I've seen people doing the first solution that came to mind to find out later that it didn't solve their problem or took a lot more effort than expected.

 Invest time in deeply understanding the impediment before taking action to solve it. Once you really know what is happening it becomes much easier to do something about it.

You need to prevent jumping into solutions too soon. Facilitation can help people to take time to understand their problems and defer or suspend judgment.

 Facilitators guide people through their problem-solving process. When people jump into action too soon, the facilitator can reflect this to them and check if they know enough about the problem before starting to look for solutions.

Liberating Structures can be used to explore problems and create a shared understanding. Examples are troika consulting, fishbowl, conversation cafe, wise crowds, and what, so what, now what.

Decide as a Team

I see teams going back and forth seemingly unable to decide what to do. Everybody throws in ideas which makes it even more difficult to choose one because other people might feel that the suggested solution is not good.

Don't take things too personally. In the teams that I work in, I make clear that it doesn't matter who comes up with an idea. It's more important to solve problems so that the team can continue.

In great teams, people build solutions by taking an idea and extending and refining it, making it better together.

It's seldom the case that one idea results in the final complete solution; instead, through discussion and iteration of ideas, improvements, and working practices, team members can build upon each other.

Good teamwork leads to great ideas that teams create and own.

To address indecisiveness, teams can agree on what techniques to use to decide. Techniques can include consensus, fist of 5, majority vote, rights to veto, etc.

Don't Try to Change Everything at Once

At times there can be multiple problems that you need to solve or multiple actions that you have to do. You would like to get everything done as soon as possible, but trying to change everything at the same time often backfires.

Teams and organizations are limited in how much change they can absorb. When they start to become overloaded, chances are high that everything stalls.

For one organization that I worked with I used a Kanban approach for managing the flow of organization change. There was a maximum number of changes that would be ongoing at the same time. When a new change was needed, an ongoing initiative either was finished or halted.

Limiting work in progress helps you to focus. In this case, it's focusing on the few problems that need to be solved first and ensure that you solve them before addressing other problems.

Keep a list of the problems that you are working on. Visualizing what needs to be solved now helps people to focus.

When doing an experiment, preferably you want to isolate it from other changes to have a better insight into the impact. Only changing one thing to find out if the situation improves, stays the same, or becomes worse.

Keep experiments small and finish them before starting new ones. Stop starting, start finishing.

Listen to Each Other

There might be team members who refuse to do what the team has agreed. Either they will object and say that they won't do it or they will passively ignore it.

If there are people who show signs of resistance when actions need to be done, by all means talk with them and listen to what they have to say. They might have good reasons for doing that. Take them seriously, ask them why and how they see things, and how they feel about it.

When I started on a new project as a coach, I felt resistance from the project manager to changes that had to be implemented in his project. I spoke with him, and instead of trying to convince him, I asked him why he resisted? He mentioned his reasons for opposing, which I welcomed very much. At first, he acted surprised. "Why don't you tell me that my project has to do the changes ordered by senior management?" I told him what the intentions were behind the changes, why the management team requested them. And explained that I wanted to understand his objections. "I'm assuming that your reasons to object to the changes are valid, the better I understand them, the more I can help the project!"

Create a culture where people listen to people and where their concerns are seriously considered. Use their feedback to improve the team's solution, or to look for a better one.

Appreciate honesty from people, it is better than expecting them to go along with a decision that they do not really believe in.

Manage Your Impediments

If there's an impediment, when would you like to have it solved? Preferably, as soon as possible.

 Give high priority to solving impediments. As long as the impediment exists, you are incurring waste. You are losing time and money. The sooner the impediment is gone, the better it is.

When you solve impediments on short notice, then managing them becomes easier. What works is to create a task to solve the impediment, include that task as part of the work to be done, and do it.

 If you are using Scrum or Kanban, then put the task on your task board. You can include an expedite lane on your Scrum or Kanban board to give them the highest priority and ensure that all work stops to first solve the impediment.

There will be situations where other activities take precedence over solving impediments. In such cases, there might be more than one impediment that needs to be worked on, where you need a system to manage impediment solving.

One possibility is to create an impediment board. This board is only used for managing your impediments. For the columns, having "to do", "in progress", and "done" should work in most cases.

Managers, Support Your Teams

Teams new to agile might initially be depending too much on decisions or actions from their managers. They are used to being told what to do and scared to do something that their managers might disagree with. They might not want to take responsibility.

I ask managers to give space to teams and individuals. I tell them to support teams in taking decisions and actions, don't tell them what to do.

If you as a manager don't give space to people, then they will be less engaged. Chances are high that they resist your decisions because they feel left out.

Managers should stand with people when things go wrong. Even if you expect that something will fail, as a manager it's better to support people to try out their ideas for themselves and get better in what they are doing by learning from their own experience.

In my workshops I teach that "the team is always right, even if they are wrong". I see Scrum masters and managers who try to push their teams to go into a direction which they believe is the right one, to find out that team members resist. Often it works better to agree on a goal and ask the team how they want to get there and what they are willing to do.

Organize for Continuous Improvement

Work is becoming more and more fragmented, which leads to a permanent state of action. People rarely take time to stop and reflect on what helps and what hinders them in their daily work.

 Continuous improvement needs to be "designed" into the way of working.

Improvement starts with a mindset of being eager to learn about how things are going and willing to take action where needed.

 My suggestion is to help people in self-assessing their effectiveness in dealing with impediments.

The book The Technology Takers proposes to set up a Change Management Function (CMF) for continuous improvement.

 I disagree that change always has to start from the top, but there should be support for improvement up to the highest organizational level.

You can collect data on impediments identified over time and the actions that have been taken. This data can help you to explore any trends and find out how effective you are in dealing with impediments.

 My book Continuous Improvement provides suggestions that you can use in your daily work to improve continuously and increase team and organizational agility.

Handling Impediments Effectively

Agile emphasizes establishing self-organizing teams and giving them whatever they need to do their work. This chapter has explored how teams can increase their effectiveness in dealing with impediments that will happen in their daily work.

Improving your effectiveness, be it dealing with impediments or any other activity, is never done. It's always possible to improve. But don't let that stop you from taking the first step.

Take the first step of your improvement journey today. Pick one thing that you feel you can do better, do it, and improve it.

Agile Coaching Tools for Impediments

Agile coaching tools are digital products that you can download and print out. These are exercises, coaching cards, and games, that I use myself in my workshops and advice work.

You can use them to coach professionals, teams, and organizations in improving their performance and the value that they deliver.

 Download agile coaching tools for a nominal fee directly from BenLinders.com/shop. Use them to coach professionals, teams, and organizations in improving their performance and the value that they deliver.

The book Problem? What Problem? has been first released on Leanpub.

 The full package of Problem? What Problem? on Leanpub includes both the Impediment Coaching Cards and the Impediment Board Game.

Agile Impediments Coaching Tools

 Teams and organizations use the Impediment Coaching Cards to improve their impediment handling skills and learn how to apply agile practices effectively.

Practice how to recognize and analyze impediments, understand how they hinder your team, and decide what to do and who can take appropriate action by deploying agile and lean principles and good practices.

 Teams use the Impediment Board Game to learn how to collaboratively recognize and deal with impediments and improve their impediment handling skills.

The game uses concepts from gamification to create an environment where teams practice recognizing and analyzing impediments. By discussing impediments they increase their understanding of how they hinder the team. Next, they learn to decide what they can do and who can take appropriate action by deploying agile and lean principles and good practices.

 Register your book to get access to supporting materials and download agile coaching tools for dealing with impediments with a discount at benlinders.com/problem-what-problem.

Training and Support

There are several ways to get trained on solving impediments: Remote training or coaching or public or in-house workshops.

My training and coaching sessions are highly interactive. You'll learn things that you can apply directly in your daily work.

 I provide Free Lifetime Support on everything that I do and all products sold on my website to help you use what I deliver in your specific situation. Register your book to receive Free Lifetime Support at benlinders.com/problem-what-problem.

Remote Training and Coaching

Remote training, mentoring, and coaching are one-on-one intensive sessions on a topic of your choice. You get just-in-time maximum value with limited time investment.

For remote coaching, I use video and audio connection (Skype, Hangout, or likewise). You get materials upfront to prepare for a session and get support from me after the session.

Workshops

I provide workshops, master classes, and training sessions, where people gain new insights, try out practices and techniques, and learn to apply them effectively in their own specific situation.

In the workshop Making Agile Work for You you will learn how to apply agile practices to develop the right products, deliver faster, increase quality, and become a happy high-performing team!

The workshop Improving Organizational Agility teaches you how to apply agile throughout your organization by changing the culture, mindset, and improve in small but meaningful steps.

In the Workshop Valuable Agile Retrospectives for Teams you will practice different kinds of retrospectives and learn how to adapt and apply retrospectives in your own organization.

Doing it yourself and reflecting, that is the way people learn new practices and develop skills in my workshops. For up to date information about my workshops, please visit benlinders.com/workshops.

Agility Assessments

I can help you to assess your agility and increase value delivered:

- In-house workshops playing the Agile Self-assessment Game.
- Public workshops that include the Agile Self-assessment Game.
- Facilitated self-assessments for teams or the organization.
- Remote or on-site training for facilitating self-assessments.
- Facilitating assessments at your event (conference, meetup, hackathon, game lab, etc.).
- Tailoring the Agile Self-assessment Game to specific needs

I'm a senior adviser and coach with more than thirty years of experience in software development and management. I'm there to guide you through your agile journey and help you increase your agility to deliver more value to your customers and stakeholders.

For the latest information about my self-assessment services, see Assessing your Agility.

About the Author

Ben Linders: Trainer / Coach / Adviser / Author / Speaker

Ben Linders is an Independent Consultant in Agile, Lean, Quality, and Continuous Improvement, based in The Netherlands.

Author of Getting Value out of Agile Retrospectives, Waardevolle Agile Retrospectives, What Drives Quality, The Agile Self-assessment Game, Problem? What Problem? and Continuous Improvement. Creator of many Agile Coaching Tools, for example, the Agile Self-assessment Game.

Ben is a well-known speaker and author; he's much respected for sharing his experiences and helping others share theirs. His books and games are translated into more than 12 languages and are used by professionals in teams and organizations all around the world.

What I do

I'm a one-person company doing many different things to help people, teams, and companies become better in developing and delivering high-quality software products and services.

In my books, workshops, advice, and coaching sessions, I focus on adopting agile ways of working, increasing agility, dealing with impediments, collaboration and communication, continuous improvement, and keeping retrospectives valuable.

I'm a practical person who wants to have a real impact and make the world a little bit better. I look for ways to apply things, share experiences, and help people experiment and learn.

I share my experiences in a bilingual blog (Dutch and English), as an editor for Culture and Methods at InfoQ, and as an expert in communities like Computable, Quora, DZone, and TechTarget.

You can follow me on twitter: @BenLinders or contact me by email: benlinders@gmail.com.

Bibliography

My Blog and Books

Ben Linders - Sharing my Experience - www.benlinders.com

Getting Value out of Agile Retrospectives - A Toolbox of Retrospective Exercise

What Drives Quality - A Deep Dive into Software Quality with Practical Solutions for Delivering High-Quality Products

The Agile Self-assessment Game - The Agile Coaching Tool For Improving Your Agility

Problem? What Problem? - Dealing Effectively with Impediments using Agile Thinking and Practices

Continuous Improvement - A toolbox for Scrum masters and Agile Coaches to increase agility

Tools for Root Cause Analysis

Register your copy of this book at benlinders.com/problem-what-problem/

Books (Ordered on Title)

Creating Great Teams - How Self-Selection Lets People Excel by Sandy Mamoli and David Mole.

Create Your Successful Agile Project by Johanna Rothman.

iTeam: Putting the 'I' Back into Team by William E. Perry.

The Lean Startup - How Constant Innovation Creates Radically Successful Businesses by Eric Ries.

The Secrets of Consulting by Jerry Weinberg.

The Technology Takers by Jens P. Flanding, Genevieve M. Grabman, and Sheila Q. Cox.

Value Planning by Tom Gilb.

Links

Manifesto for Agile Software Development

Agile Self-assessment Game

Agile Self-assessment Tools and Checklists

Agile Coaching Tools